Scenes and Monologues for Urban Youth

Pannell

REAL

Scenes and Monologues for Urban Youth

By Pannell

Limelight Editions
New York

First Limelight Edition   August 2002

For production rights, contact Mark Wright, Executive Artistic Director,
Theatre Unbounded, 117 Cumberland Avenue, Syracuse, NY 13210;
(315) 475-4671

Interior design by Nancy Davidson

Manufactured in the United States of America

Library of Congress Cataloging-in-Publication Data

Pannell, Lynn.
Real : scenes and monologues for urban youth / by Lynn Pannell.
    v. cm.
Contents: Dolls—Sista-Sistah—In trouble again—Dreamin'—
Cousins—Brotherly Love—Flirtation—Ain't life a trip—Karen—
Best friends—Jason—Girlfriends—Star—Playground incident—
Tomorrow—Crazed—No secret—Critical—No way out—Parlor—Lost.
        ISBN 0-87910-973-4
        1. Monologues—Juvenile literature. 2. Children's plays,
American. 3. Acting—Juvenile literature.
    [1. Monologues. 2. Acting.] I. Title.
PN2080 .P33 2002
812 ' .6—dc21
                                                        2002007599

Introduction

Throughout my career, teaching theatre arts and acting to youth in community centers, public and arts schools, I have always found it difficult—or close to impossible—to find a scene-study book suited, or even relevant, to the populations of the classes I teach. Hence, this book is born out of necessity: a collection of scenes and monologues that are real and plausible to the young person who lives in urban America, who faces serious issues everyday, and who needs his or her voice heard.

"Real": Scenes and Monologues for Urban Youth speaks to the issues of today's youth—issues such as teen pregnancy, family abuse, gang violence, love, sexual behavior and dreams, to name only a few. Divided into monologues and two-, three-, or four-person dialogues, the scenes are arranged in chronological order according to age, from scenes for younger children to scenes for pre-teens and teens.

In 1999, I received a small but welcome grant from the Cultural Resources Council of Onondaga County, New York, that afforded me the writing time to complete the project. Though the trust of the grant was to create a tool for theatre-arts instructors, this book is not limited to that audience. Counselors, group leaders, and teachers working with urban youth will all find this book useful as a means of involving young people in discussions important to their lives.

I want to thank the following people for their support, encouragement and friendship: Mark Wright, Onondaga Cultural Resources Council; my son and daughter, Keusi L. Pannell and Alexis MacArthur; my mother and sister, Lee and Maggie Pannell; Aunt Delphia, Valerie and Tristian, Nuru Sala, Oloya Tyehimba, Tunura Barbour, Valerie Woods, Dorothy Randall-Gray, Pamela Bass, Katya Wilson, and Mel Zerman, for having the insight to publish this work.

Thank you all—Pannell.

CONTENTS

DOLLS

MOLLY
8 years old, is playing with her dolls on the stoop.

KESHA
8 years old, enters jumping rope.

KESHA

Hey, Molly.

MOLLY

Hey, Kesha.

KESHA

What you doin'?

MOLLY

Playin'.

KESHA

Why you always playin' with dolls?

MOLLY

I like dolls.

KESHA

Yeah, I like dolls too, but you don't see me playin' with them all the time.

MOLLY

So!

KESHA

So, nothin'. Don't you ever want to play somethin' else?

MOLLY

No. Like what?

KESHA

I don't know.

MOLLY

Sometimes, I play wrestlin' with my brother.

KESHA

Oh, yeah? I like wrestlin' too.

MOLLY

But I like my dolls best.

KESHA

Why?

MOLLY

I don't know.

KESHA

That's funny.

MOLLY

What's funny?

KESHA

That you don't know why you like playing with dolls so much.

MOLLY

I guess, I like it 'cause I can make them do anything I want.

KESHA

Like what?

MOLLY

Like anything.

KESHA

Com'on tell me.

MOLLY

I can make them dance, like this, see.

KESHA

That's wack.

MOLLY

Is not. I can make them fight...make them kiss...
anything I want.

KESHA

How many dolls you got, anyway?

MOLLY

I don't know, a lot.

KESHA

Yeah, what's a lot?

MOLLY

Let me see, I got four here, and then there's Pie-pie,
Anna, Ken, Barbie, Sally, Janet...

KESHA

Dag, that's a lot of dolls.

MOLLY

Yeah, I guess, but there's this one I saw, when me and
my Momma was at the store. She was so beautiful. She
had long blond hair and came with curlers and everything.

KESHA

You got any black dolls?

MOLLY

No.

KESHA

How come?

MOLLY

I don't know. Nobody ever bought me none.

KESHA

Not even your grandmother?

MOLLY

No. She don't like dolls. She said, "Young girls don't need to be playin' with no baby dolls. Only makes them want to have a real one."

KESHA

You wanna have a baby?

MOLLY

No, you crazy! I just like playin' with my dolls.

6 7 8 9 10 11 12 13 14 15 16 17 18

SISTA, SISTAH!

YOLANDA (YOYO)
is 11 years old, fair complexion with long hair.

TINY
is 8 years old, very dark in complexion with short hair.

HELEN
is a group leader.

TINY

She makes me sick.

YOYO

You make me sick!

TINY

Nobody's talkin' to you.

YOYO

Yeah, but you talkin' 'bout me!

HELEN

All right, you two. Enough's enough. What do I have to do to get you two to get along?

TINY

You ain't got to do nothin'.

HELEN

Look, Tiny, I took the two of you out of group to try to come up with a solution to your problem.

YOYO

I ain't got no problem.

TINY

You is the problem! Always actin' like you betta than everybody else. Think you cute 'cause you got long hair!

YOYO

I am cute!

TINY

See, she got a stink attitude! That's why nobody likes her.

YOYO

I ain't got no stink attitude.

HELEN

"I ain't got," Yolanda!

YOYO

You know what I mean. She be messin' with me all the time.

TINY

I mess with you 'cause you easy to mess with.

HELEN

So, you're saying you pick on her just on G.P.

YOYO

G.P.?

HELEN

General Principles.

TINY

No, not just on G.P.....she be always gettin' in my bizness.

YOYO

I do not!

TINY

Do too!

YOYO

Do not!!

HELEN

All right! How does she get in your "bizness," Tiny.

TINY

Okay, right...we was doin' art and she says, "You should use green for the grass" and I told her to mind her bizness, if I wanted green grass I would have used green paint. I didn't want green grass...I wanted what I had.

YOYO

Who ever heard of pink grass?! That's stupid.

TINY

You stupid!!

HELEN

So, what you're telling me...is that you started fighting over the color of grass?

YOYO

I was tryin' to help her. She act like, me helpin' her is gonna hurt her.

TINY

Don't nobody need your help!

YOYO

Must do, if they gonna make grass pink!

TINY

What makes you think I need your help?! You the one in the fifth grade and on second grade reading level.

YOYO

Shut up before I smack you.

TINY

Who you gonna smack?! I ain't scared of you!

HELEN

All right, girls, enough.

TINY

Ain't no enough. I'm gonna yank that stank hair right out of her head!

YOYO

Do it and I'll smack the black off of you!

TINY goes after YOYO, HELEN steps between them.

HELEN

That's it! You sit over there and Tiny you sit here! I can't believe this! This goes much deeper than the color of grass?! The two of you need to take a good long look at yourselves. And recognize what's really going on here.

Silence. Beat. The girls glare at each other.

YOYO

She hates me.

HELEN

Why does she hate you, Yolanda?

YOYO

I don't know...she just does.

HELEN

Why do you hate Yolanda, Tiny?

TINY

'Cause she always tryin' to take what is mine!

YOYO

What?!? I don't be takin' nothin' that's yours.

TINY

Yeah you do.

HELEN

What has she taken of yours, Tiny?

TINY

Everything.

HELEN

What are you really trying to say?

TINY

Just that. Everything. Things be fine till she come. Then everything changes. People treat me different 'cause she come. They don't see me when she's around. And I don't understand it. I'm ten times smarter than her. But all they see is her. Why is that?!

YOYO

I don't know, why...but I see you...and sometimes I wish I could be you.

IN TROUBLE AGAIN

SHANTAY

10 years old, sits in the school office.

SHANTAY

I try to be good...but it always seems like no matter what I do, I'm gettin' in trouble. Like today, I was mindin' my own business, playin' tag with Reggie and Marcus. When out of nowhere Jaquin steps up and pushes me down. Talkin' about I said somethin' about him. I ain't said nothin' about Jaquin. I may have thought it, but I didn't say nothin'. And I told him so as I got up off the ground. Don't you know he pushes me again. But this time I stepped back and as he fell forward I punched him in the stomach. You would have thought I stabbed him or somethin' the way he was screamin.' And wouldn't you know it, Mr. Douglas was standin' right there, but all he saw was me punch Jaquin in the stomach. Dag, that's why I'm sittin' here in the principal's office now. I don't know why things like this always happen to me. I don't be botherin' nobody. Last time, Principal Meecham said she was gonna suspend me from school if I got in trouble again. Mr. Douglas said they should put me in that school for "violent" kids. Shoot, I ain't "violent." I'm just not gonna let somebody come up and mess with me. What they think I'm suppose to do?! Man, Momma's not gonna believe me this time. She'll probably put me on punishment for the rest of my life and call my Dad. He most likely will tell me to forget about them Air Jordans. Dag...I can't wait till I see that Jaquin again. Got me in all this trouble. I ought to really talk about him now.

6 7 8 9 **10** 11 **12** 13 14 15 16 17 18

HAMPTON

is 12 years old. He plays basketball.

SISSY

is Hampton's sister. She is 10 years old.

HAMPTON

I got game, baby. Got me a serious crossover. Can't
nobody stop this! Drive right, cut left and sky for the
dunk! Ughh! And one! Yeah, baby! If the middle shuts
down. Pass off to the wing. Run the baseline around to
the top of the key. Catch the pass and shoot the J!
Swoosh!! *(HAMPTON makes crowd cheer sounds).*
There's 20 seconds left on the clock, Dick and the
Hoyas are down by three. Coach has called a timeout.
No better time for a timeout, Tom. This is what it's all
about, baby. The final four. A clutch time for clutch
players, baby. What's coach telling his troops right now,
Dick? He's telling them to get the ball to Hampton.
Hampton has been the Hoyas' go to man since the
beginning of the season. You know they got to rely on

him now, baby. Let's go Hoyas! Let's go Hoyas! Let's go Hoyas! This crowd is going wild, baby. Coach has Hampton in-bounding the ball. He passes to Smith and Hampton runs across court to the far wing. Jackson, the defensive guard for Duke, is sticking to him like glue, baby. Duke is playing a box and one. The Hoyas swing the ball around the perimeter. Ten seconds left. Smith sets a pick for Hampton. He crosses to the opposite corner. Steps behind the three point line. Williams feeds him a beautiful bounce pass. Five seconds left. Hampton cradles the pass and in one smooth motion he takes the shot. *(beat)* Swissh! Three! *(HAMPTON makes crowd cheers sounds.)* The crowd goes wild! The Hoyas have tied the game! Overtime, baby. We're going into overtime! It don't get any better than this, baby. Hampton the clutch man does it again!!!

SISSY

Jamie! Jamie! Hampton!

HAMPTON

What?! Don't you see I'm doin' somethin'?

SISSY

Momma said, "Come in and finish your homework!"

HAMPTON

Arrr, Man...I got to play the overtime!

SISSY

She said "Right now!" Besides...how you gonna play
for the Hoyas if you don't get through junior high
school first?

HAMPTON

Shut up.

HAMPTON exits. SISSY picks up the basketball.

SISSY

Shamika Hampton steps to the free throw line. No time
left on the clock. She makes this free throw and the
New York Liberty will win their first WNBA
championship. There's a hush over the crowd. Hampton
wipes her brow. Studies the rim. She bounces the ball
once, twice, three times, takes a deep breath and shoots!
Swoosh! New York Wins! The crowd goes wild!!

*SISSY makes crowd cheer sounds as she jumps up
and down.*

VOICE (O.S.)

Shamika Hampton, get in here.

SISSY

Yes, mam...I'm comin', Momma.

6 7 8 9 10 11 12 13 14 15 16 17 18

COUSINS

HAKIM
is 12 years old.

BOBBY
is 15 years old.

HAKIM has just witnessed his cousin BOBBY sell a bag of drugs on the street.

HAKIM
Hey Cuz...what are you doin'?

BOBBY
Get on out of here, Hakim, man. You know your Momma don't want you hangin' round me.

HAKIM
Yeah, I see why!

BOBBY
Whatchu talkin' about, bro?

HAKIM
I saw you pass a bag and take cash from that car that just drove off.

BOBBY grabs HAKIM.

BOBBY

Listen here man, you better mind your business.

HAKIM

It is my business. You're my cousin, Bobby.

BOBBY pushes him away.

BOBBY

Get out of my face.

HAKIM

No! You know what you're doing is wrong.

BOBBY

Don't talk to me 'bout wrong. You ain't nothin' but a kid.

HAKIM

I may be a kid but I'm not stupid.

BOBBY

You gettin' on my nerves, Hakim.

HAKIM

Good. Man, Bobby, think about what you're doing.

BOBBY

PAYIN' THE RENT, Brother! Look at you wearin'
them brand X clothes. The only decent clothes you
got I bought!!

HAKIM

That's weak, man. Momma says, "Clothes don't make
the man."

BOBBY

Well, Aunt Jackie don't know ev'rythin'.

HAKIM

Nobody said she did!

*A car pulls up to the curb where BOBBY and
HAKIM are arguing.*

BOBBY

Yo, what's up? Got what you need.

HAKIM

No he doesn't, Mister. Besides, you don't want a kid
seeing you buy drugs, do you?!

The car pulls off.

BOBBY

Damn it, Hakim! I'm gonna kick your butt!

HAKIM

You got to catch me first.

BOBBY gives chase as HAKIM "shakes and bakes" his way out of BOBBY's grasp.

BOBBY

You little punk! If I ever get my hands on you…you'll be sorry!

HAKIM

Not as sorry as you'll be when your Momma finds out what you're doing!!

BOBBY

My Momma already knows chump! Who you think is paying the bills.

This stops HAKIM in his tracks. BOBBY grabs him.

HAKIM

I don't care if Aunty knows. It's wrong, Bobby and you know it! You could go to jail, man!

HAKIM breaks BOBBY's grip.

BOBBY

Jail don't scare me.

HAKIM

Yeah, right. I don't care what you say. You're my cousin, my blood, and I can't just stand around and let you mess up your life.

BOBBY

You just don't get it, do you?!! This is my *life*!

HAKIM

Not if I got anything to say about it.

Another car pulls up to the curb. HAKIM gets to the car before BOBBY.

HAKIM

He's out of business. Drive on, man.

BOBBY

Shut up!

HAKIM shouts as he struggles to keep BOBBY back from the car.

HAKIM

I'm going to memorize your license plate and call the police!

*The car pulls off. BOBBY pushes HAKIM to the
ground. He kneels over him with his fist raised.*

BOBBY

I'm gonna punch your lights out, punk!

HAKIM

Go ahead, hit me...but I'm going to be here everyday,
doing the same thing each time until you stop.

*BOBBY's fist is paused above HAKIM's head.
BOBBY hesitates.*

HAKIM

It's wrong, Bobby. It's wrong, Cuz.

BOBBY

I know...but what else am I supposed to do?

BROTHERLY LOVE

JJ *and* ***KK***
twin brothers, age 13, are in their bedroom.

KK, born first, is considered the older of the two.

JJ

You make me sick.

KK

Why? 'Cause I won't agree to your stupid plan.

JJ

It's a good plan. All we got to do is sneak in the living room, pass the kitchen and out the bathroom window. Momma will never know we're gone.

KK

That's crazy. I ain't breakin' my leg climbin' out of no bathroom window.

                              JJ

You a punk, man.

                              KK

Don't be callin' me no punk. Why don't you just ask
Momma if we can go?

                              JJ

'Cause you know what she's gonna say. "Y'all too
young to be out this late at night!"

                              KK

Maybe she's right.

                              JJ

Oh shut up, Momma's boy! You goin' with me or not?

                              KK

How we gonna get back in when we come back?

                              JJ

I don't know, we can figure that out when we get back.

                              KK

See, that's what I mean, stupid.

                              JJ

Don't be callin' me stupid. You just scared.

KK

Momma's not even asleep yet. How you figure we gonna slip pass her?

JJ

She'll be snoring in a few minutes. You know she always falls asleep watchin' TV.

KK

What we gonna do when we get outside?

JJ

Hang with Patrick and Buddy at the corner. Play some hoops. Have some fun. Who knows?

KK

You want me to sneak pass Momma, climb out the bathroom window, risk breaking my neck, so that we can hang out at the corner?!

JJ

Yeah, we'll have some fun for a change.

KK

I don't think so!

JJ

Well, forget you then.

KK

I'm goin' to bed, and if you was smart you'd do the same.

JJ

Dag KK, you just a Momma's boy. Always gotta do the right thing. You never wanna take a chance.

KK

I take chances, just not dumb ones. Man, JJ, you don't even know how we gonna get back in the house. Hangin' with Patrick and Bobby ain't worth all that.

JJ

Patrick says we can make some money.

KK

Make some money? How? *(beat)* Are you crazy JJ? Momma would seriously kick your behind.

JJ

I knew you would say that. Momma, Momma, Momma! That's all you know. That's why I want to live with Daddy.

KK

Daddy'll beat your behind, too.

JJ

No he wouldn't. He ain't like Momma. I could do

whatever I wanted to if I lived with Daddy.

KK

C'mon JJ, get real.

JJ

I'm goin'! You ain't got to go. I don't need you.

KK

You ain't goin' nowhere!

JJ

Yeah, right.

KK

I'll wake Momma up, man.

JJ

Wake her up, I don't care. I'm goin' and y'all can't stop me.

KK

You actin' real stupid, JJ.

JJ

All I want to do is have some fun. You the one makin' it all complicated and what not!

KK

I ain't makin' nothin' complicated. I'm just tryin' to show you how dumb your plan is.

JJ

Forget you, KK.

KK

Forget you too, then! I'm goin' to bed. I got one last thing to say. You wanna be down with Patrick and Buddy so bad, you willin' to risk everything, even Momma's trust in you. And that's really wack, JJ.

JJ grabs his jacket and exits towards the bathroom. KK shakes his head and pulls the covers up over himself.

Next morning. KK wakes up in a panic. Looks over at JJ's empty bed.

KK hears his mother calling for him and JJ. He hesitates, then slowly gets up. JJ enters. His clothes are rumpled and his shirt is out of his pants.

KK

How'd you get back in without Momma seeing you?

JJ

I didn't.

KK

What you mean, you didn't?

JJ

I got to the bathroom. Had the window open and everything. I was ready, man. Then I heard what you said playing over and over in my head…that thing about Momma's trust. So I sat down in the tub to think about it.

KK

So why didn't you come to bed?

JJ

Man, I thought so long and hard till I fell asleep in the tub. Dang, my neck hurts.

KK

(Laughing) JJ, you one crazy little brother. Sleepin' in the bathtub. But I'm glad you didn't go, man.

JJ

Shoot, man…I figure Momma's trust was worth more than one night of hangin' out on the corner.

KK

You got that right, bro.

6 7 8 9 10 11 12 **13** 14 15 16 17 18

FLIRTATION

DAVID, JUNIOR, and **MAMIE**
are all 13 years old.

JUNIOR

Man, look at the way she eyin' you.

DAVID

Naa, you crazy man. She ain't even lookin' at me.

JUNIOR

Yeah, she is, bro.

DAVID

So what. That don't make no difference.

JUNIOR

Yeah, it do. Make all the difference in the world, man.
When a girl be givin' you the eye, that's your chance!

Your clue to hit it quick! B'fore it gets cold, if you know what I mean.

DAVID

Man, you crazy. Mamie ain't thinkin' about me. A fine girl like her ain't got time for a regular guy like me.

JUNIOR

Man, you wrong. Fine girls always go for "regular" guys like you. Listen, I knows when a girl gots the hots for a guy. And she has been givin' you the "look" all mornin'. Check it. She's lookin' ova here right now.

DAVID

Yeah, right.

JUNIOR

Naaa, for real, man. Look, here she comes.

DAVID

Get out! She really comin' ova here?!

JUNIOR

She walkin' passed the basketball court right now, headin' this way, man.

DAVID

Oh dip. I got to go.

JUNIOR

Where you goin', blood?

DAVID

I don't know, but I go to go!

JUNIOR

Wait up, man... Is there something you not tellin' me?

DAVID

What? No!

JUNIOR

Then why you runnin'?

DAVID

I'm not runnin'! It's just that, that...I can't talk to her.

JUNIOR

Yeah, you can!

DAVID

No I can't!! You talk to her for me!

JUNIOR

No way, man. She lookin' at you, not me!

MAMIE

Hey, David.

JUNIOR

Hey, Mamie.

DAVID

Oh, hey.

MAMIE

Can I talk to you for a minute, David?

DAVID

Ughhh, I guess.

JUNIOR

I'll see you later, man.

DAVID

Where you goin?!

JUNIOR

Just ova here, bro. Chill.

DAVID

I'm cool.

MAMIE

David, why you always be ig'ing me?

DAVID

What you mean? I don't be ig'ing you.

MAMIE

Like now. You can't even look at me.

DAVID

I'm lookin'. What you want?

MAMIE

I don't want nothin'! I was just tryin' to be friendly.

DAVID

Friendly? Why?

MAMIE

Just because, that's all.

DAVID

Why you want to play me? A girl like you don't have any time for a guy like me.

MAMIE

Why you say that? What kind of girl you think I am?

DAVID

A nice girl with lots of fellas callin' her on the phone.

MAMIE

Yeah, but that don't mean nothin'.

DAVID

What you tellin' me, that you would be interested in me callin' you?!

MAMIE

Now, I didn't say all of that. I just think you're a nice guy, that's all and maybe we could be friends.

DAVID

Friends? Like me and Junior, friends?!

MAMIE

No, just friends, David. Why it got to be all that?!

DAVID

'Cause....I really like you, that's why!

MAMIE

You really like me?! Since when? I sure couldn't tell you liked me by the way you treat me.

DAVID

A guy's got to protect his heart, you know.

MAMIE

Like a girl doesn't, right?!

DAVID

No, I'm not sayin' that.

MAMIE

Just what are you trying to say, David?

DAVID

I... I... I mean...dang. Look at me, I'm sweatin', I'm nervous...all because of you.

MAMIE

There's no reason to be nervous. Shoot, you think it was easy comin' ova here to talk to you?

DAVID

I guess not. Can I ask you something?

MAMIE

We talkin', right?

DAVID

Did you like the flower I left on your locker?

MAMIE

That was you?

DAVID

Yeah.

MAMIE

And you weren't going to tell me?

DAVID

No.

MAMIE

I love the flower you left.

DAVID

Really?

MAMIE

Yeah, really.

DAVID

Cool. So you want to go out Saturday?

MAMIE

I can't. My family has plans for the weekend.

DAVID

Oh...I see...okay, right. Maybe another time, then.

MAMIE

Yeah, another time.

DAVID

I got to go.

MAMIE

Yeah, me too.

DAVID

See you around.

DAVID starts to walk away.

MAMIE

David.

DAVID

What?!

MAMIE

Want to do homework together, tonight?

DAVID

Yeah, I guess. What time?

MAMIE

Meet me at the library after school?

DAVID

Sure. See ya.

MAMIE

Yeah, see ya.

6 7 8 9 10 11 12 13 14 15 16 17 18

AIN'T LIFE A TRIP

SHARON

14 years old, is alone in her room. She is obviously upset.

SHARON

God. I wish I didn't go to that school. Momma's struggling to pay the tuition for me to go there. Why can't I just go to a public school and get lost in the crowd? Make some friends, some black friends. But nooo, she got to put me in that school with all them white kids. 'Cause she thinks I'll get a better education at that school. What a laugh. You know what happened today...that big nose Joshua had the nerve to touch my ass. I smacked the shit out of him. Then he turned around and called me a nigga! I was already mad, and that just made me go crazy. I pushed him down and started to kick him over and over again. Then Miss Cradle came out into the hall and grab me. Dragged me to the Principal's office talkin' 'bout, "You're in big trouble, young lady!" I got her big trouble. She gets me to the principal's office. I tell them what Joshua did. And I get two weeks suspension for fighting. I wasn't fighting, I was kicking the living hell out of that fool. Mr. Blume says some corny crap like "sticks and stones may break your bones but words can never harm you." Well, I'm here to tell you that words can cut deep and I'm not about to let some jerk disrespect me. The days of turning the other cheek are over. Joshua? He's got some bruised ribs and a note written home to his father. Tell me where's the justice in that?! God, I wish my Momma would take me out of that school. Seems like everyday I got to put up with some stupidity. A kid can only take but so much and today was just the last straw. Who knows? Maybe in public school the same thing could happen, but at least there'd be more than 12 black kids in the school and I'd have someone to cover my back. God, I hate that school and its lily-white pretenses. Maybe now, Momma will take me out of that school.

6 7 8 9 10 11 12 13 14 15 16 17 18

KAREN

KAREN

can be 14 to 16 years old. She is talking on the phone.

KAREN

Girl, my mother makes me sick. She won't let me do anything. I got to be home by a certain time. Can't hang out on weekdays. Saturday's are for working around the house. And don't even think about a Saturday night. Check this, she told me I couldn't have any boyfriends until I was seventeen. She must be crazy. Better yet, she just plain old fashion. Talkin' about "a nice young lady doesn't entertain young men till she is the proper age." Shee-it! Oh and let me tell you about the clothes she wants me to wear. Talkin' about wack. I mean...she must think this is the 50's or somethin'. I'm so sick of her tryin' to run my life. To prove to you how off my mother is...one minute she tellin' me I can't have any boyfriends and the next she makin' sure I know about contraceptives. I'm not talkin' about the pill, nooo, she says "givin' me birth control pills is like sayin' it's okay to have sex." Now tell me how backwards is that! I know every contraceptive there is to know about. I've been schooled on all the VDs, and AIDS is her preacher's box. Yet still, she keeps me locked up, can't go nowhere with my girls. Can't have boys callin' me on the phone. Can't go to a school dance. Can't, can't, can't!!! Shit! I'll be glad when I get grown. 'Cause as she's always sayin', "When you grown, you can do what you want, but as long as you live under my roof, you will do as I say do!" Tell me how many times have I heard that! What she don't know is that I'm gonna do what I want to do no matter what she says.

BEST FRIENDS

DEBRA and *STEPHANIE*
are both 16 years old.

DEBRA is at her best friend STEPHANIE's house.

DEBRA

What if I was to tell you that I love you.

STEPHANIE

Yeah, I love you too, Dee.

DEBRA

No, that's not what I mean. Not like a sister or a friend.

STEPHANIE

Ohh, wait a minute now...You tellin' me you funny?!

DEBRA

I'm not tellin' you anything. I was just saying *suppose* I was to tell you I love you in that way. What would you say?

STEPHANIE

I'd say get the hell out of here! But you not tellin' me *that*, right?!

DEBRA

Right.

STEPHANIE

Why you actin' all weird and what not?

DEBRA

I don't know...It's just that...forget it.

STEPHANIE

No, say what you was gonna say.

DEBRA

It's just that sometimes, I get these feelings...for girls, I mean.

STEPHANIE

What kind of "feelings," Dee?

DEBRA

I don't know how to explain it. They're just feelings.

STEPHANIE

Romantic feelings?

DEBRA

Sometimes. Like yesterday, in gym...I was minding my own business, when Sheila brushed passed me and accidentally touched me, you know.

STEPHANIE

How she gonna "accidentally" touch you?

DEBRA

I don't know, she just did, okay!

STEPHANIE

Okay...so what happened?

DEBRA

Nothin' happened. I just had these feelings when it happened. Scared the crap out of me too. I had never been turned on by a girl before.

STEPHANIE

Turned on?! Now you're scaring me, Debra.

DEBRA

I know. But it happened. And I think Sheila knew it too, 'cause she looked at me and smiled this freakin' wicked smile.

STEPHANIE

You talkin' about Sheila Mason? From history?

DEBRA

Yeah, she smiled and I got even more turned on.

STEPHANIE

Oh my God, Debra. Are you crazy? Are you weird or something? What's wrong with you, girl?!

DEBRA

Why it got to be all that?! I'm just tellin' you what happened. I didn't say I liked it!

STEPHANIE

Well, you did say it "turned" you on. Shit. What am I suppose to think?! Okay, so what are you gonna do about it?

DEBRA

Nothin'. It probably won't happen again. Besides, I like Josh.

STEPHANIE

Josh, huh? Ever get those "feelings" when Josh smiles at you?

DEBRA

Well...no.

STEPHANIE

I don't know, Dee...It sounds to me, like you got a serious problem.

DEBRA

Why it got to be a "problem"?!

STEPHANIE

'Cause, you know, girl! It ain't natural.

DEBRA

Why isn't it natural? I mean, I know more about me, a girl, than I know about boys.

STEPHANIE

Wait! Hold up! Are you sayin', you think you gay?

DEBRA

No, I'm not sayin' that! I'm just being honest with you, my best friend. If I can't be honest with you who else I'm gonna be honest with?

STEPHANIE

I got cha. But are you being honest with yo'self?

DEBRA

Forget you, Stephanie. I'm goin' to sleep.

STEPHANIE

Huh, huh. Sleep. Well, all I know is, if you are gay, it don't make no never mind to me. You still my best friend.

DEBRA

Thanks, Steph. I'll remember that.

STEPHANIE

No problem, girl, no problem.

JASON

JASON

is 17 or 18 years old. He is well built and very manly in appearance.

JASON

I'm here, 'cause...I can't live at home any more.
You see, my father found me out. I wanted to tell him a
long time ago, but I didn't have the nerve...the heart.
Guess, I knew how he would react. So instead, I got all
"A's" on my report cards. Went to church every Sunday.
Did my chores like he said to do. Made MVP on the
Football squad last season. I played defensive end. I can
hit, hit harder than most on the football field. Nothing
gets passed me. Sacked the Quarterback three times and
made four interceptions in the championship game. I
was *the man.* Even worked this jive part-time job to
keep money in my pocket. But all of that wasn't enough
for him. The hardest thing about all of this is, that I've
fought it all my life. Prayed so hard that it wouldn't be
true. But it is and I am. Ashamed? A little, I guess. Not

because I am but because I wasn't man enough to say it out loud. Friends? I've only got a couple I can truly trust. Not many would understand where I'm comin' from. So, here I am. Living on my own. Sneaking phone calls to my Momma, 'cause no matter what she still loves me. But him...he won't even look at me. Yelled at the top of his lungs "You ain't no son of mine!" In some ways, I guess I wanted to be found out. I was getting real tired of hiding. Tired of pretending. What am I gonna do? Finish my senior year, get accepted to a Division One school. Graduate and go Pro. Oh...what am I gonna do about that other thing. I don't know. Maybe I'll "outgrow" it. That's what Momma thinks. Maybe I'll bury it deep inside somewhere and never let it out again. Or maybe I'll just let it be.

6 | 7 | 8 | 9 | 10 | 11 | 12 | 13 | 14 | 15 | **16** | **17** | 18

GIRLFRIENDS

RHEA
is 17 years old.

JACKIE, LIZ, *and* ***TYRA***
are all 16 years old.

They are coming in from school.

TYRA

Dag y'all, can't you wait till I get the key out of the door?

JACKIE

Excuse me, but I've got to go to the bathroom.

JACKIE exits.

RHEA

That girl always got to pee.

LIZ

Tyra, what you got to eat?

TYRA

Liz, if you don't get out of my mother's refrigerator—

LIZ

I'm hungry. Please, Ty?

RHEA

Why you always beggin'?

LIZ

Tyra, you need to talk to your friend.

TYRA

Look, don't y'all be startin' nothin' up in my house.

RHEA

I ain't startin' nothin'. She was beggin'.

LIZ

No, I wasn't! I just asked my girl for somethin' to eat. What business is it of yours, anyway?

RHEA

I'll make it my business if you keep messin' with me.

LIZ

Oou big bad Rhea, I'm so scared!

TYRA

I'll make some sandwiches, so we all can have somethin' to eat.

LIZ

Sounds good to me.

JACKIE enters from bathroom.

JACKIE

Did I hear food?

RHEA

God, the two of you are just alike.

JACKIE & LIZ

That's right, baby. That's how sistahs are.

TYRA

Sisters?!

RHEA

How y'all gonna be sisters?! You black and she white.

LIZ

Color don't matter. It's what you feel, you know!

JACKIE

That's right! Sistahs from the heart!

RHEA

Oh please! Ty, where's the remote? I don't want to listen to this nonsense!

TYRA

No TV, Rhea. You said you were going to do my hair.

RHEA

You ready? No!

TYRA

I got to get my comb and stuff.

JACKIE

If she don't do it, I will, Tyra.

RHEA

Yeah, right. You can't even do your own hair. What do you call that hair style?

LIZ

You want me to make the sandwiches, Ty?

JACKIE

It's called "Fly girl"!

LIZ

Awesome.

RHEA

I don't even have time for you, Jackie.

JACKIE

You wish you could look as good, Rhea.

LIZ

You tell her, girl.

LIZ exits to the kitchen.

RHEA

Whatever.

TYRA

Liz, don't you mess up my mother's kitchen. I'll be right back.

TYRA exits.

JACKIE

What's wrong with you?

RHEA

Nothin's wrong with me. What's wrong with you?

JACKIE

You know I was only playin'. Why you got all this attitude?

RHEA

What attitude?!

JACKIE

That one, right there! You actin' like somebody did something to you.

RHEA

Like you care.

JACKIE

Yeah, I do care about your sorry behind. You know you my girl, Rhea.

RHEA

Yeah, just like Liz, right!

JACKIE

Oh no, you didn't. You jealous...

RHEA

I am not jealous. It's just so phony.

JACKIE

Phony?! Why you don't like Liz? She's cool.

RHEA

Right. She's cool.

JACKIE

You just don't like white people, that's all.

RHEA

They ain't never give me no reason to like them.

TYRA enters with comb, brush and other hair products.

TYRA

Okay, I've got everything. Comb, brush, hair, rubber bands. You ready?

RHEA

Yeah, get a pillow.

TYRA takes one the pillows from the couch. She places it on the floor in front of RHEA and sits down.

JACKIE

Ty, what do you think of Liz?

TYRA

She cool.

JACKIE

See, I told you. Even Tyra thinks she's cool.

TYRA

What?

JACKIE

Rhea trippin', girl. She don't like Liz 'cause she white.

RHEA

I didn't say I don't like her. I said she phony.

JACKIE

No, what she said was white people ain't give her no reason to like them.

RHEA

That's right.

JACKIE

That is so stupid, Rhea.

RHEA

Don't be callin' me stupid. You just lettin' her hang with you 'cause you think it makes you white.

JACKIE

What?! Listen to yo'self girl. As black as I am, I'm tryin' to be white?! Get real.

RHEA

I am being "real." And Liz is just hangin' with you so she can get to date some black guys.

TYRA

Hey, that's my head you jerkin' Rhea.

RHEA

Sorry, Ty.

JACKIE

Oh, that is so stupid. You just pissed 'cause Bryant was talkin' to her instead of you, today.

RHEA

So what if I am. Them white girls are always tryin' to take our men.

TYRA

Girl, can't nobody take nobody. Brothers go that way 'cause they want to.

RHEA

No, they go that way 'cause the white girls be givin' up the hoochi.

JACKIE

Like sistahs don't? Rhea, you got problems, girl.

RHEA

I ain't got the problem. You the one with the problem tryin' to be white with your black ass.

JACKIE

See...you gonna make me hurt you.

TYRA

Yo! Chill y'all!

RHEA

She the one that better chill. Before I get up from here and make her check herself.

JACKIE

Right. I'd like to see you try.

TYRA

This is crazy! Why are y'all wastin' your time arguin' about Liz?

LIZ enters carrying a plate of sandwiches. All become silent. LIZ stares at them. RHEA looks away.

LIZ

I better go.

JACKIE

You don't have to leave, Liz. Rhea is just actin' wack. What she said don't mean nothin'.

LIZ

No, I don't want to be the one that breaks up y'alls' friendship.

RHEA

Okay, here we go...the great martyr act. Girl, you ain't all that!

LIZ

I'm not tryin' to be. I just thought it would be nice to have some girls to hang with.

RHEA

Yeah, right!

LIZ

You know, Rhea, I don't know why you don't like me?! I didn't do nothin' to you.

RHEA

Yeah, you did.

LIZ

What?! What did I do to you?!

JACKIE

You was talkin' to Bryant, today.

RHEA

Forget you, Jackie.

JACKIE

Forget you! With your prejudice ass.

TYRA

Stop it, y'all. Liz, listen…

LIZ

It's okay, Ty. This is the same mess I went through with my white friends 'cause I was hangin' with you guys. I'm out of here.

JACKIE

Wait, I'll go with you.

LIZ

For your information Rhea, I was talkin' to Bryant this afternoon about you. He was askin' me if I thought you liked him. Later.

LIZ exits.

JACKIE

See, you so stupid. Later Tyra.

JACKIE exits. TYRA looks at RHEA with disappointment.

RHEA

What?!

TYRA

You know, what?!

RHEA

You want me to do your hair or not? 'Cause I'm out if you don't.

TYRA

Ree, you got to fix this.

RHEA

I ain't got to fix nothin'! Let them go, I don't care.

TYRA

Well, that's a problem 'cause I do.

RHEA

Then you fix it. I'll talk to you later.

RHEA exits. TYRA shakes her head in disbelief.

STAR

STAR

*is 16 years old. She appears to be in control, but
internally she is falling apart. She talks to her mirror
image as she puts on her makeup.*

STAR

Do you know how hard it is, not be stressed out? There
is so much to stress over. Some really silly things, like
your hair, your clothes, nails, shoes. But then there's
serious things too. Like, grades, getting into the right
school, money, living up to my parents expectations. My
teachers' expectations. Will I be successful for them?
For me? Will I ever get out and be somebody? Or will I
be trapped here forever? Trapped in this mundane
existence. Fighting off the roaches, you know, eight and
two legged ones. Sometimes, just getting up in the
morning makes me feel like…I don't know…Like I'm
taking a closer step towards death? Yeah, I know, I'm
just a teen. I'm not supposed to be thinking about death.
Just life, right?! But you know, you can't think about life
without thinking about death. Sometimes I think I think

too much. Which only adds to the stress in my head. Because, you see, there's always more questions than answers. You want to know what I do with my stress? I dance. I take eight dance classes a week. I sweat, my body aches and sometimes I'm so tired I can't even think. I lay in my bed awake, late at night, when I should be sleeping, thinking about the next question. Will I be good enough? Did I work hard enough? Am I too fat? Can I lose ten more pounds? Should I audition or not? Am I good enough? Am I great enough? Do I have that special something? I want to be a star! It's my dream to go to Broadway. Be discovered. Sing and dance my way into fame and fortune. Get out of this place with its dungeons of pissy hallways and forgotten souls. But you know, the most messed up thing about my dream? Is that my dream is my greatest stress. Why? 'Cause it may only be a dream.

PLAYGROUND INCIDENT

MYRA
is 16 years old.

CARLOS
her brother, is 15 years old.
They sit together on a bench in the playground.

JAMES
16 years old, enters later.

MYRA

Carlos, do you think I'm fat?

CARLOS

Nooo chica, you are just filled out a little.

MYRA

Ay dios mio, man...what do you mean filled out a little?

CARLOS

You know. More womanly. *(beat)* Sometimes I worry 'bout you being so, too.

MYRA

Worry? Why?

CARLOS

You know. All these muchacos be smellin' 'round you.
I see them.

MYRA

Don't nobody be smellin' around me!

CARLOS

Oh yeah. I see them.

MYRA

Who? Who you see?

CARLOS

Never mind who. If I catch any of them, you'll know.

MYRA

You my little brother, not my father, man.

CARLOS

Well Popi's not here and I'm in charge.

MYRA

(Under her breath) Gonyo. Go home Carlos, I don't
need you here, talkin' like that.

CARLOS

I'll go home when I'm ready. *(beat)* Who you waitin' for?

MYRA

Nobody.

CARLOS

I swear, if you waitin' for that negra!

MYRA

What you talkin' 'bout "negra"?! You negra too!

CARLOS

I'm Puerto Rican and don't try to change the subject.
You waitin' for that black kid, right?!

MYRA

What if I am? You can't do nothin' about it!

CARLOS

I can do plenty! Me and my boys can do plenty!

MYRA

Your "boys"?! A bunch of punks! Pickin' on people for
no reason.

CARLOS

Hey! Don't be dissin' my boys! We take care of our
neighborhood. And if that negra comes 'round here, we
take care of him, too!

MYRA

You so tough! Talkin' 'bout takin' care of somebody. You don't know how to take care of anyone, not even yourself!

CARLOS raises his fist as if to hit MYRA. He hesitates.

CARLOS

You betta be glad you my hermana. All I know is, that before Popi left he told me to watch out for you and Mommie and that's what I'm doin' .

MYRA

Yea, you takin' so good care of me and Mommie, that's why she cry at night 'cause you takin' so good care of us. You doin' nothing but makin' trouble. Don't you see that? Stayin' out late. Not goin' to school. Hangin' with "yo' boys" doin' who knows what. If Popi was here he snatch you by your neck!

CARLOS

Shut up!

JAMES enters. He wears glasses. He carries a school book and pad.

JAMES

Hey, what's up?

CARLOS

What you doin' here, man?

MYRA

Hola, James.

CARLOS

I asked you a question, chump!

JAMES

What's with him?

CARLOS

I'm talkin' to you, negra!

JAMES

Yo man, you best chill.

CARLOS

I got yo' chill negra!

MYRA

Carlos, stop it! Com'on, James, let's go.

CARLOS

What you think you doin'? You think you can just come in here and walk off wid my sista? You think you bad or something?!

MYRA

Carlos, gonyo, man. Stop it!

CARLOS

Shut up, Myra! I'm talkin' to this punk ass!

JAMES

Okay…I don't know what your problem is but…

CARLOS

You the problem, negra, you!

JAMES

Look man, back off before someone gets hurt.

CARLOS

The only person that's gonna get hurt is you, mudda!

CARLOS pulls a knife and lunges for JAMES. They struggle. MYRA screams. CARLOS falls to the ground, he is bent over in pain. JAMES stands with the knife in his hand. He is in shock. The knife falls to the ground. MYRA goes to her brother and pulls him into her arms.

MYRA

Oh God, Carlos, why?!

TOMORROW

DERRICK

*can be 16 to 18 years old. He is streetwise and
resourceful.*

DERRICK

What's the point?! I mean, you bust your butt tryin' to
do the right thing and what do you get? No money in
your pocket and a pat on the head. That's all my daddy
ever got. And it wasn't much different for my momma
either. So what's the point in tryin'? In dreamin'? We all
know what happens to people who dream. Me?! I'm
livin' today for *today.* Ain't nothin' promised. And even
if it was, promises are always being broken. So I say
live life for today. Do what you got to do to get by and
when it don't work your way keep gettin' up. They
always be handin' you that line. "Get a good education,
son." But what they be teachin' in school don't have
nothin' to do with me. And I don't know how to make it
mine. How to make what they're teachin' important
enough to remember. Important enough to make a

difference in my life. You know what? Education is for the educated. And whether you go to school in a building or in the streets the lessons are the same. Take what you need and leave the rest behind. Plans? Plan what? How you gonna die? How many women you gonna have? What you gonna eat for breakfast if you see mornin'? Don't make sense to plan. The way things are right now, plannin' is a fool's fancy. Right now? Just stayin' alive is the feature presentation, baby. I mean, between the spray of bullets from drive-bys, justice's searching my drawers and the job of getting a job. It's a wonder a young black man like me is even around to talk about tomorrow much less plan for it.

6 7 8 9 10 11 12 13 14 15 16 17 18

CRAZED

SHEILA and TEDDY
in their mid to late teens.

They are in a lover's embrace. The caress becomes too
passionate and SHEILA breaks away.

TEDDY

What?!

SHEILA

I think we better stop.

TEDDY

Dag girl, it was only a kiss.

SHEILA

Yeah, and you know where a kiss can lead.

TEDDY

No...I don't! Seein' as all we ever do is kiss! *(beat)* Arr,
com'on girl. You know you the only one for me.

SHEILA

Is that right?!

TEDDY

Damn straight! My heart belongs only to you.

SHEILA

And it better stay that way too!

TEDDY

No doubt, baby! You know I'm crazy about you.

SHEILA

Teddy, I love you, but...

TEDDY

Hey…no "but"s. I love you too, girl. And sometimes I just want to show you how much. Com'ere, girl.

A passionate embrace. Once again SHEILA breaks away from the passion of their caress.

TEDDY

Arr, com'on, baby...don't do this to me!

SHEILA

What!?! Don't you do this to me!!

TEDDY

What's your problem?! You scared or somethin'?!!

SHEILA

No, I'm not scared! I'm just tryin' to hold on to what I believe!!

TEDDY

And what's that!? You gonna save it till you married?!

SHEILA

Maybe I just will!

TEDDY

God, Shelia, that is so lame!

SHEILA

Forget you, Teddy!

TEDDY

Naw…You the only girl in our school who's not down with the program.

SHEILA

That's not true.

TEDDY

Oh, yeah, it is. All the girls in yo' crew is givin' it up, but you! I know.

SHEILA

How do you know?

TEDDY

Don't worry about how I know. I just know, awright!

SHEILA

Well, that's their business. I don't have to be like them.

TEDDY

You right. You don't have to be like them. But I got to be real wid you, baby. I'm a man, and a man's got needs.

SHEILA

You a man?!

TEDDY

That's right! Bonafide All American Male, babee!

SHEILA

Since you a man, bonafide and what not. Let me ask you one thing?

TEDDY

Ask away, baby.

SHEILA

You really love me or you just want to get in my pants?

TEDDY

What kinda question is that?!

SHEILA

A honest one, wantin' an honest answer.

TEDDY

Well, you know the answer.

SHEILA

If I knew the answer I wouldn't have asked the question.

TEDDY

Why you askin' me stupid questions? You know I love you.

SHEILA

No, I don't know. I thought you did but the way you actin' makes me question.

TEDDY

The way I'm actin'?! How about how you be actin'? Lettin' me feel you up and what not. Get all hot and bothered, then you say "No! Stop!" like you some kid and shit.

SHEILA

Maybe I am a kid. And one day I'll be a woman. And it doesn't matter how much I love you or you love me. I'm not doin' that till I'm ready.

TEDDY

Well, when the hell you gonna be ready, Sheila?

SHEILA

Who knows, maybe never. Maybe when I meet a real man. One who can respect my feelings.

TEDDY

Yeah, well, I need a woman who can respect my feelings.

SHEILA

Yeah? Well, that must not be me.

NO SECRET

MONA
is 15 years old, but she looks much older.

MONA

I'm fifteen…yeah, I know I look older but that's just the way it is. Let me tell you, somethin'…until a couple of months ago, I was livin' high. Had me a Sugar Daddy, baby. He'd pick me up from school in his Lexus. Silver and black it was. Take me wherever I wanted to go. Bought me the finest clothes and made sure my Momma had food on the table. Whatever I wanted, he got for me. I mean I was in love, girl. And he said he loved me, too. Yeah, it was true love. He even told me that I was the best thing that ever happened to him. That his wife didn't know nothin' compared to me. She come around tryin' to get loud with me in the street, but I just ignored her sorry ass. He told me he was gonna divorce her and marry me when I was old enough. Girl, I was happier than I'd ever been before. Didn't have no time for them high school *boys*. Had me a real man. Money, jewelry and clothes to boot. He even went to church one Sunday with me and my Momma. Everybody at church thought he was with Momma, but I let them know right away that he was with me. You should have seen the way them old biddies was lookin' at me and him. I didn't care, I had my man and they had theirs to get. Anyway, two months ago, I was gettin' real sick in the mornings. Couldn't keep nothin' down on my stomach, you know. Momma took me to the doctor. Yep, I was pregnant. I just knew he was gonna be happy for us. When I told him, he jumped up and said,"You sure it's my baby?" My heart sank, like in mud and for the first time since meeting him I felt dirty. You see, I really thought he loved me. Thought that having a man was the real deal. Thought that with a man everythin' would be all right. God, no one told me that he wasn't a real man. No one told me that I had to become a real woman first. Yeah, well to make a long story short…I ain't seen him since.

CRITICAL

MARSHA
is 17 years old.

MALIK
is her boyfriend. He is 18 years old.

MALIK
I don't know what you want me to say.

MARSHA
How about, "Don't worry, baby. It'll be all right."

MALIK
Funny. This is serious and you're makin' jokes.

MARSHA
Well, you know what they say...

MALIK
Yeah, okay. So, what do you want to do?

MARSHA

If I knew that I wouldn't have called you.

MALIK

Well, whatever you decide is okay by me.

MARSHA

Whatever I decide?! I didn't do this on my own. So why should I be the one who has to decide what happens next?!

MALIK

I'm just sayin'...I'll help no matter what.

MARSHA

Help? I think you've helped enough, don't you?!

MALIK

I mean...I'm not gonna be like other guys.

MARSHA

Well, that's good to hear. What do you want me to do?

MALIK

I don't know. I mean...I got plans and this wasn't one of them. I mean...

MARSHA

We both had plans, remember?! I got a future too, you know. You're not the only one ready to make something of himself.

MALIK

Nobody said you don't have a future. Look, let's not fight. We need to be calm and figure out what we are going to do.

MARSHA

Right. You think we should tell our parents?

MALIK

Ohhh damn, my mother will have a shit fit!

MARSHA

Your mother? Mine...I don't even want to think about what my mother will do!

MALIK

I hear that. Well, if we don't tell them and they find out, we'll be in worse trouble.

MARSHA

Yeah...I just can't see myself doing this now.

MALIK

What are you saying?

MARSHA

Just what I said. I can't see myself having a baby now. You know, I see my friends who got babies, on the bus and what not. The baby be cryin', or they got dirty faces, or they look hungry…and my friends look tired. And they act like they don't care. I mean, I know they care but they seem so helpless. They can't go no place. Except to pick up their WIC checks. I don't want it to be like that. I want…

MALIK

I know, you want the baby to have what you have. Be protected, loved, nourished and cared for.

MARSHA

Yeah, I don't want my baby to want for anything. But how can we do that when we're still in school? Working at Micky D's can't take care of a family.

MALIK

So what you saying? You want to get an abortion?

MARSHA

No, that's against God…to take a life that way.

MALIK

Yeah, I know, but…we'll lose two lives if you don't. We'll lose our lives. Listen, Marsha, I don't want to be an absent father. I don't want my son or daughter to have to grow up wondering why his daddy ain't around, just like I did. And I'm not just talking about the physical. I'm talkin' about the…the…emotional…the…

MARSHA

Don't go gettin' deep on me, Malik, okay. Keep it simple, please.

MALIK

All I'm saying, baby, is how can I be there for him and you if I'm out there workin' two and three jobs 'cause I'm not qualified for one good job. I mean, I know being a father is more than just putting food on the table. It's about being there. Knowin' what's up with your kids. Seein' them through the good times and the bad. Tell me, how can I be a good father if I'm never home. And I'll never be home 'cause I'll be workin' all the time just to keep a roof over our heads and food on the table. I don't want it to be like that. I want us to be a real family. You know, dinner at seven, everyone around the table, talkin' and what not. Finding out what's goin' on with each other. If it can't be like that…then what will we have?

MARSHA

I don't know, Malik. Not a family, that's for sure. You know somethin', Malik, I'm scared…

MALIK

Me too, baby…me too.

6 7 8 9 10 11 12 13 14 15 16 17 18

NO WAY OUT

CHERI
16 years old, stands on the roof's edge.

TAMIKA
17 years old, enters.

TAMIKA

Hey Cheri, girl, you up here?! You missin' the jam, girl. Cheri! Where are you? Oh my God…

CHERI

Don't come up here, Tamika.

TAMIKA

You don't have to worry about me comin' up there on that ledge. Girl, what is wrong with you?!

CHERI

Nothing's wrong with me. Just leave me alone.

TAMIKA

There must be something wrong with you! You standing on the edge of the freakin' roof!

CHERI

Don't make me laugh, T.

TAMIKA

I'm not trying to make you laugh, girl. Come on down from there, Cheri. Let's talk about it.

CHERI

There's nothing to talk about. I'm tired of talking and nobody listening.

TAMIKA

Arr, Cheri, come on. This is stupid.

CHERI

So now I'm stupid too, right?!

TAMIKA

No! You're not stupid. But standing on the edge of the roof is.

CHERI

Forget you, T.

TAMIKA

Cheri, bring your behind down from there before…

TAMIKA goes to grab CHERI.

CHERI

Don't! I'll jump, I swear. Don't you come any closer.
I swear, I'll jump!

TAMIKA

Okay, okay.

CHERI

I'm so sick of people telling me what to do. Just leave
me alone, T.

TAMIKA

I can't. You expect me to just stand here and let you kill
yourself? Com'on Cheri, you have too much to live for.

CHERI

Right now, I can only think of reasons why I should
step off this roof.

TAMIKA

No! Wait! Okay, I'll give you a reason to come down
from there. Tomorrow's another day and things can only
get better?

CHERI

Yeah right, Tamika. Another day to live through the same
crazy ass shit I've been dealing with for all of my life.

TAMIKA

God, Cheri, we all have to live through the madness!
You're no different from anyone else. You don't see me
tryin' to kill myself.

CHERI

No, but you different than me. You stronger than me.
You got someone to live for. You got your mother,
father, sisters and brothers. Me?! Who I got to live for?!
A father who tries to be a lover. A mother who acts like
she doesn't see it at all. And friends who make fun of
me 'cause I'm not perfect like them, right!?!

TAMIKA

No one said you had to be perfect. None of us are
perfect. Damn, Cheri, don't do this.

CHERI

Don't do what?! Put an end to this misery. You know the
other day was almost a perfect day. I was cool. Looked
good and no one at school had messed with me all day.
Then I get home and Wham! The shit just fell apart.

TAMIKA

What are you talking about?

CHERI

It must be my fault, right?! Who else's fault could it be?
Not Momma's. Not his. He's the one that puts clothes

on my back and food on the table. He's the one that hands out the punishment. He's the one who loves me, right?! Oh God, help me end this!

TAMIKA

Cheri! No! Don't! If you do this then he will win. He will get away with all he's done and your mother won't have to face the truth…and I will lose my closest friend. Please, don't do this…let me help you.

CHERI

You can't help me T, no one can.

TAMIKA

You, Cheri. Only, you can help yourself. Stop blaming yourself. It's not your fault. Believe me, you can do something about him damn it!

CHERI

Do what?! He's my father!!

CHERI breaks down and cries. TAMIKA grabs her from the edge of the roof and rocks her in her arms.

6 7 8 9 10 11 12 13 14 15 16 17 18

PARLOR

MARLON
is 16 years old.

TANK and SMOKEY
are both 17 years old.

ROCKY
16 years old, lays in a coffin.

MARLON sits alone in the funeral parlor. He weeps
quietly to himself.

MARLON

Man, it wasn't suppose to be like this. We had plans,
bro. You was gonna be the king and I the prince. We
were gonna set things straight. Hook up the neighborhood. Move Duke and his crew out. Make good on our
promises to our moms and pops. Take care of business.
But look at you now…gone. And I'm left here to do it
all alone. That ain't right, Rock. You just had to go and
hang out with Tank and Smokey. Man, I told you not to
go with them clowns, damn.

TANK and SMOKEY enter.

SMOKEY

Dang, it's quiet in here, man.

TANK

It's a funeral home, fool. Dead people don't make noise.

SMOKEY

I know that.

TANK

Where is everybody?

SMOKEY

It's still early.

TANK

Can't be that early, we here. What time is this thing 'pose to start, man?

SMOKE

Who knows, but I'll be glad when it do. All them fine biddies be up in this mud—you know, showin' grief and what not. Needin' a shoulder to cry on. And I got big shoulders…

TANK

That's sick, Smoke, man. We here to pay our respects to a fallen brother and you thinkin' about hittin' on women at the funeral.

SMOKE

Hey, whatever works, man.

TANK

I don't believe you sometimes, man.

SMOKEY

Whatever.

TANK

Hey, look at Rocky, man. All laid out in his finest.
Lookin' all peaceful and shit.

SMOKEY

Yeah, he does look peaceful. There's that punk Marlon,
man. Yo, Marlon!

TANK

Leave him alone, Smoke. He's mournin' the loss of his
best friend.

SMOKEY

Yeah, you right.

TANK

You know, Rock told me, Marlon saved his life when
they was kids.

SMOKE

Oh yeah? I don't see how, man. Marlon is such a
chump, man.

TANK

Chump or not, that's what Rock said.

SMOKEY

I guess that's why Rocky was always standin' up for him.

TANK

You better believe it, bro.

SMOKEY

It was cold, how they took Rock out, man.

TANK

It was worst than cold, man. It was wicked unjustified. They had no reason to ice Rock, man.

SMOKEY

You know, we can't let this go unanswered. We got to retaliate!

TANK

You got that right!

MARLON *(to ROCKY)*

Man, I told you, hangin' with them gang bangers was gonna get you dead. But no, you wouldn't listen to me. Always had to do things your way. Why, Rock? Did you think we wouldn't need you? Did you think you was invincible? What about your family, man? Peanut has run off somewhere. Can't nobody find him. Your girl, Ree, looks bad, man. She says she doesn't even want to have the baby. What's suppose to happen now, man? What am I suppose to do? Why didn't you listen to me, Rock. Why, why?

SMOKEY

Listen to him, Tank, man. He's ova there cryin' and what not.

TANK

Leave the boy alone, Smoke—

SMOKEY

You would think he'd be out there lookin' for the ones who did his partner. Instead, he's in here cryin' like some sorry ho.

TANK

Leave it alone, man.

SMOKEY

Naa, I'm just sayin'. If it was you. I damn sure wouldn't be in here cryin'! I'd be out poppin' the one who popped you, you know what I mean.

TANK

Yeah, I gotcha.

SMOKEY

Yo, Marlon!

TANK

Don't mess with him, Smoke.

SMOKEY

I'm just goin' to talk to the chump! Yo, Marlon! Yo!
Man, this chump trying to ignore me or what?!

TANK

Leave it alone, Smoke. I'm tellin' you, somethin' don't
feel right 'bout this.

SMOKE

Naaa, he hear me callin' him. Yo, Marlon! Punk, you
better listen up. Don't make me have to come ova there.
You believe this, man?! I'm gonna have to hurt this kid.
Actin' like he don't hear me.

ROCKY

He don't!

SMOKEY

Who said that?

TANK

Sounded like Rock, man.

SMOKEY

Get out of here, Rock's dead, man.

TANK

No man, this is freak. That was definitely Rock's voice.

SMOKEY

What you talkin' 'bout fool. Look Rock is laid out in that coffin ova there!

ROCKY sits up.

TANK

Oh, sheeit, man, look!

ROCKY

What's up, partners?!

SMOKEY & TANK

Oh dip!

TANK

Naaa, stuff like this only happens in the movies, man.

SMOKEY

Well, we ain't at the movies, bro.

ROCKY

Now, what was that you was saying about hurting my bud?

SMOKEY

Nothin' man, nothin'.

ROCKY

I didn't think so. You know, Marlon's right. If I had listen to him I wouldn't be here with you clowns.

TANK

What do you mean, here with us?!

ROCKY

You figure it out.

MARLON *(to ROCKY)*

Man, why did you have to be so like so many others? We were suppose to be different. Had a better plan than what they planned for us. We wasn't suppose to end up a statistic of black on black violence, man. We was suppose to survive, man. Make it through the shit. Not give in to their game. God, I wish you could get up out of that coffin, Rock. Get up! Get up! So that I can kick your ass!

SMOKEY

He is up, fool! Look, he's standin' right there.

TANK

How come we see you and he don't?

ROCKY

You ain't figure it out yet, man.

TANK

You mean...

SMOKEY

Naa, he don't mean that!

ROCKY

Yeah, I do.

TANK & SMOKEY

Ohh, man...

MARLON

Damn, I miss you, Rock.

ROCKY

Don't worry bro, I'll always be by your side.

6 | 7 | 8 | 9 | 10 | 11 | 12 | 13 | 14 | 15 | 16 | 17 | 18

LOST

TREVOR, JAY and **PETE**
are in their mid to late teens.

They are in a basement one-room apartment. TREVOR sits with his hands in his pockets. JAY stands, looking out of the window. PETE nervously guards the door.

JAY

Listen up. We gotta lay low here, till it's dark.

PETE

Man, this is crazy.

JAY

Calm down, Pete, man.

PETE

I am calm. I didn't plan on gettin' caught up in this shit, no way. But look at me. Stuck here in the middle with you guys.

JAY

Step off, Pete. You was down from the beginning, and you know it.

PETE

Man, I didn't know he was really goin' to do it!

JAY

Yeah, well, it's done now. And there's nothin' we can do about it.

PETE

Man, I didn't even know he had a gun!

JAY

You need to shut up! Nobody wants to hear you whine. Can't think with you bustin' at the mouth.

PETE

I gotta get out of here, man.

JAY

Sit down, man, please.

TREVOR

Mr. Brian, man, he never shoulda said what he said, man.

JAY

Don't worry, Trev, we'll figure something out, relax.

TREVOR

Naaw, he deserved what he got, man.

JAY

It's okay, Trevor, man.

TREVOR

He was always pickin' on me, man. Callin' me names
and what not. Dissin' me in front of everybody, all
the time.

PETE

Man, Mr. Brian was a jerk! He picked on everybody,
not just you.

TREVOR

What do you know about, white boy?! I ain't never hear
him call you no nigga!

PETE

Oh, I see, now I'm a white boy?! Been your friend since
we was four, but now I'm a white boy!!!

TREVOR

That's right, nigga! You's a white boy! What do you
know about it!

JAY

Chill, Trev!!

PETE

Look, if that's how he feels, then I'm outta here! I don't need this shit!

JAY

Pete, you know he's not right. Like you said, we've all been friends since we was four. You can't just walk out on him, us.

PETE

Oh no?! Watch me!

JAY grabs hold of PETE's arm. PETE knocks his hand away and starts for the door. TREVOR blocks the door.

TREVOR

Where you think you goin!?!

PETE

Home, man! I'm goin' home. I don't want no part of this.

TREVOR

You not slick. I know you goin' to the cops.

PETE

Naw, man. You talkin' crazy. Listen, I'm goin' home, bro.

TREVOR

You lyin'. I can always tell when you lyin'.

PETE

Yo, Jay? Talk to this fool, man.

TREVOR pushes PETE down. TREVOR steps over him.

TREVOR

I'll take you out, right here!!

JAY

Trev, man. Trevor, chill! We don't need to be fightin' amongst ourselves, now. Take it easy, brother. You know Pete, he's our home boy. He wouldn't do nothin' to hurt us. Isn't that right, Pete?

PETE

Hell, yeah, that's right! I don't know what Trevor is thinkin', man.

TREVOR moves from over PETE and goes back to sit on the couch. PETE, clearly shaken, gets up from the floor.

JAY

Okay. Listen up, we got to get Trevor out of here. Send him somewhere. Trev, you got family somewhere?

PETE

How we gonna do that, man? I'm flat broke. You got cash?

JAY

Yeah, I got fifty bucks.

PETE

Fifty bucks? Man, that'll get him to the corner and back.

JAY

We'll just have to get some more, then.

PETE

Where from? You gonna take up a collection and what not?

JAY

Shut up, Pete.

PETE

This is crazy, Jay. Man, we can't help him.

JAY

Shut up! We gotta help him, don't you see. If we let them catch him, our asses are cooked.

TREVOR

He had no right, man. He shoulda never step up on me like that. What was I supposed to do?

PETE

Walk away! That's what you should have done! Just walked away, Trevor, damn.

TREVOR

Wasn't no walkin' away, Pete. I'd been walkin' away for too long.

PETE

What is he talkin' about? Walkin' away for too long.

JAY

Man, we all had it in for Mr. Brian.

PETE

Yeah, I know, but…

TREVOR

But nothin'. He got what he deserved.

PETE

And what do we got, Trev? Hiding out in a hole. Scared to show our faces. Our folks worried and goin' crazy. God, I know my momma's freakin' about now.

JAY

Yeah, you not the only one with a momma. Think about Ms. Greene, Trevor's moms. She must be truly goin' over the edge.

PETE

You right. So what we gonna do?

JAY

There's a bus to upstate, at one. We wait till then. Get him a one-way ticket and keep our mouths shut.

PETE

Upstate where?

JAY

Newburg. I got a cousin, up there. I'll call him and tell him to look out for him.

PETE

I don't know, man. How we gonna get him to the bus station without being seen?

JAY

Let's worry about that later, okay.

TREVOR

I'm not runnin'. I did it and I'm glad I did it. He got what he deserved.

JAY

Trev, you not thinkin' straight. You can't go to jail, man. You'll never make it in jail.

TREVOR

Maybe not, but it don't make sense to run.